AngularJS

An Ultimate Guide on Web Application Development 3rd edition

By Daniel Green

Disclaimer

While all attempts have been made to verify the information provided in this book, the author doesn't assume any responsibility for errors, omissions, or contrary interpretations of the subject matter contained within. **The information provided in this book is for educational and entertainment purposes only. The reader is responsible for his or her own actions and the author does not accept any responsibilities for any liabilities or damages, real or perceived, resulting from the use of this information.**

The trademarks that are used are without any consent, and the publication of the trademark is without permission or backing by the trademark owner. All trademarks and brands within this book are for clarifying purposes only and are the owned by the owners themselves, not affiliated with this document.

Table of Contents

Book Description   5

Introduction   8

Chapter 1: Definition   9

Chapter 2:How to create Components   14

Chapter 3: How to create forms in AngularJS 2   29

Chapter 4: Directives   41

Chapter 5: Views   49

Chapter 6: Expressions in AngularJS 2   57

Chapter 7: Filters   60

Chapter 8: Controllers   71

Chapter 9: Services   76

Chapter 10: Tables   83

Chapter 11: HTML DOM   90

Chapter 12: Includes   96

Chapter 13: Modules   103

Chapter 14: Scopes   113

Chapter 15: Custom Directives   120

Chapter 16: Dependency Injection   128

Conclusion   141

Book Description

This book discusses the AngularJS 2 framework which belongs to Javascript. The book begins by explaining what the framework is, and where it is used. The book then explores components, including how to develop the different parts of the components. AngularJS 2 brought about much change to the framework as far as the structure of forms is concerned. This book will guide you on how to use the framework so as to develop forms.

You will learn to understand the three layers which define forms in this framework. You will also learn how to create various form controls using this framework. Directives are also explored in detail, so you will learn how to use these so as to start your application, create the variable or the model to be used in the application, and to initialize the data to be used in the application.

Views, which define the UI (User Interface) of your application, are covered, with instructions on how to develop them. have been discussed, We need to bind the data for the application to the HTML. This is the purpose of expressions. These are discussed in this book, showing you how to use them in this framework. Filters re used to display a subset of the data, and you will be taught how to apply these on an array or a collection.

The following topics are explored in this book:

- Definition
- How to create Components
- How to create forms in AngularJS 2
- Directives
- Views
- Expressions in AngularJS 2
- Filters
- Controllers
- Services

- Tables

- HTML DOM

- Includes

- Modules

- Scopes

- Custom Directives

- Dependency Injection

Introduction

AngularJS, just like the other Javascript frameworks, is a very useful framework for web developers. The framework is aimed at helping developers to create dynamic web pages for an application. Most people usually use devices with small screens so as to access the web. Examples of devices include mobile phones, PDAs, and tablets. This means that we need to develop web pages which can be supported on these devices. This is why the Javascript development team introduced the AngularJS 2 framework which assists developers in creating or developing mobile apps. This book will help you to learn this framework with much ease.

Chapter 1: Definition

AngularJS is a structural framework used by programmers for the development of dynamic web pages. With this framework, the programmer uses the HTML as the template, and makes it possible for them to express the components of their applications more clearly by extending the syntax provided by HTML. The framework is also small in size, about 60KB. By extending the vocabulary, which is used in HTML, they make the programmers' code much more readable.

The framework is also highly compatible with other Javascript frameworks, such as the EmberJS, and it is easy to add extra features to it so as to achieve your goals. The framework also provides the developers with numerous Javascript libraries which help them to achieve their goals. With this framework, both the data and the views are kept in sync, meaning that the developer will not have to manipulate the DOM elements manually. Web pages which have been developed by the use of this framework exhibit a high degree of compatibility with any kind of web browser.

Recently, the Javascript development team released AngularJS 2, which is a framework which is used for the development of mobile apps. It can also be used for the development of web apps.

The AngularJS 2 framework was written to support both ES6 and ES5. It highly relies on components, which includes both the views and the controllers for the app. With the view, we get the template which provides us with how the web page will look. The controller is responsible for determining the behavior of the web app. In this book, we will explore the AngularJS 2 framework in detail.

First Program in AngularJS 2

Let us begin by creating our *"Hello name"* app in AngularJS 2. Just create a file, and then add the following code to it:

@Component({

selector: 'example'

})

@Template({

// let us bind the input element to our control object which is

```
// which has been defined in the class component

inline:        `<input    [control]="username">Hello
{{username.value}}!`,

directives: [forms]

})

classExample {

constructor() {

this.username = new Control('Name');

}

}
```

Once you have written the code, just run it. You will notice the
following output:

Hello:

Just type your name in the text field, and then press the "*Enter*" key. You will notice the following output:

Hello Mike!

As shown in the figure above, I have provided the name "*Mike*" into the text field.

Chapter 2:
How to create Components

Those who were used to Angular 1.x are aware of directives. In AngularJS 2, we have the components. We said that the components are   made up of the views and the controllers. The view provides the user interface, or the template, whereas the controller will determine the behavior of Javascript.

Most people think that AngularJS 2 does not have the controller part, but this is only because it is part of the component. To demonstrate how a component looks, we will create one for a better understanding. Remember that we said that AngularJS 2 is supported in both ECMAScript 6 and ECMAScript 5.

Navigate to the root directory, and then create a new file.

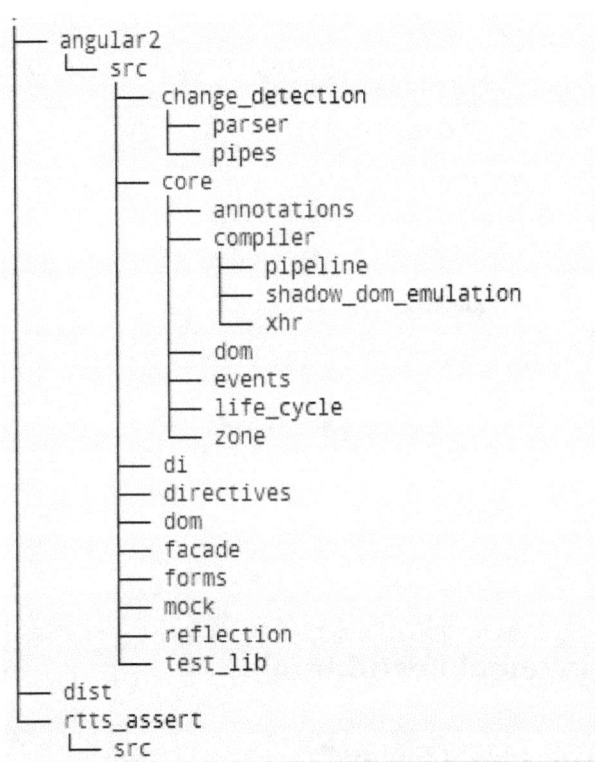

```
├── angular2
│   └── src
│       ├── change_detection
│       │   ├── parser
│       │   └── pipes
│       ├── core
│       │   ├── annotations
│       │   ├── compiler
│       │   │   ├── pipeline
│       │   │   ├── shadow_dom_emulation
│       │   │   └── xhr
│       │   ├── dom
│       │   ├── events
│       │   ├── life_cycle
│       │   └── zone
│       ├── di
│       ├── directives
│       ├── dom
│       ├── facade
│       ├── forms
│       ├── mock
│       ├── reflection
│       └── test_lib
├── dist
└── rtts_assert
    └── src
```

Give it the name *"Td.es6."* With the extension, it is very clear that we will follow the syntax provided by ES6. However, if you are not comfortable with the extension, just use the old one, that is, *".js,"* and all will be well. Add the following code to the file:

import {Component, Template, bootstrap,Foreach} from 'angular2/angular2';

import {TodoStore} from 'services/TodoStore';

```
@Component({

    selector: 'td-app',

    componentServices: [

        TodoStore

]

})

@Template({

    url: 'templates/td.html',

    directives: [Foreach]

})

class TdApp {

    tdStore : TdStore;

    constructor(tdStore: TdStore) {

        this.tdStore = tdStore;

}

add($event,newtd){
```

```
        if($event.which === 13){

        this.tdStore.add(newtd.value);

                newtd.value = '';

}

}

toggleTdState(td){

        td.done = !td.done;

}

}

bootstrap(TdApp);
```

With the first two lines of the above code, we have imported the components which belong to ES6. The first line of code has imported the component, "template", "forEach", and "bootstrap". These have been imported from the "angular2/angular2" modules. In the second line, we have imported the custom service "TodoStore", and the importation has been done from the "Service/TodoStore" modules.

In the next step, we wanted to create a controller for our component. It will have the name "TdApp", and then a class can be created as follows:

```
class TdApp{

}
```

Notice the use of some annotations in the class. These include the following:

@component- this will signify that the app *"TdApp"* is a component. The property *"selector"* specifies the HTML selector for our component. *"componentServices"* specifies what our component will rely or depend on. Notice that we have only one service to rely on, and we will create it very shortly.

@template- this specifies the template that our app should use. In our case, we will use the template *"template/td.html"* for our application. The specified URL should lead to the location where we have stored the template. The property *"directives"* will specify the directives that our component uses. Note that these are needed by the template, rather than the whole of the component. However, only one directive will be needed by our template, that is, the *"forEach"* directive.

We should then add a constructor to the app. This can be done as shown below:

```
constructor(tdStore: TdStore) {

    this.tdStore = tdStore;

}
```

How to create the Service

In the *"services"* directory, just create a new file and give it the name *"TdStore.js."*Notice the use of the *".js"* extension in the name of the file. Add the following content to the file:

```
export class TdStore {

    constructor(){

        this.tdList = [];

}
```

```
    add(it){


this.tdList.unshift({text:it,done:false});


}


}
```

The "*TdStore*" is a normal Javascript class. We have given it a single method named "*add()*", and a constructor.

The constructor is responsible for creating an array which can be used for holding the items that we specify. To display these items, we have used a list in the template. Each time that we are to create a new item in the array, we will call the "*add()*" method. Once the item has been created, it is added to the array. We then use the "*done()*" method to check on whether this was successful or not. Once this is done, we use the "*export*" keyword so as to export the class.

How to create template

Navigate to the directory *"templates,"* and then create a new file. Give the file the name *"td.html."* Add the following content to the file:

<style>

    @import

url(http://maxcdn.bootstrapcdn.com/bootstrap/**3.3.4**/ css/bootstrap.min.css);

    @import

url(http://fonts.googleapis.com/css?family=Open+Sans);

</style>

<style>

.container{

    font-family: 'Open Sans', sans-serif;

      margin-top: 190px;

```
}

.done{

        text-decoration: line-through;

        color : #998899;

}

        .bottom-offset{

        margin-bottom: 19px;

}

</style>

<div class="container">

        <div class="row">

                <div class="col-xs-4 col-xs-offset-4">

                        <div class="bottom-offset">

                                <input          type="text"
class="form-control"          placeholder="Add
something to this field" autofocus #newtd
(keyup)="add($event,newtd)"/>
```

```html
</div>

<div *foreach="#td in tdStore.tdList">

        <input type="checkbox"
    [checked]="td.done"
    (click)="toggleTdState(td)"/> <span
    [class.done]="td.done">{{td.text}}</span>

</div>

</div>

        <div class="col-xs-4"></div>

</div>

</div>
```

We have imported both the Google fonts and Bootstrap. We have also created stylesheets, and then referred to them by use of the annotation "*@import.*" The custom CSS rules for our template have been placed inside the <style> tag. It is also possible for you to write the CSS file separately, and then do the importation to the template. Our template has two parts, that is, a text field which takes input from the users, and a text area having the list of the items which we specify.

The text field has been created as follows:

```
<div class="bottom-offset">

        <input type="text" classs="form-control"
        placeholder="Add something to this field"
        autofocus #newtd
        (keyup)="add($event,newtd)"/>

</div>
```

This will give out the following:

```
Add something to this fie
```

"Index.html" file

The final step involves creating this file, and then loading it to the main module. Note that it should be created in the root directory. It should have the following content:

```
<html>

<head>

<title>Angular 2 App</title>

<script src="/dist/es6-shim.js"></script>

</head>

<body>

<todo-app>Starting up...</todo-app>

<script>

System.paths = {

'angular2/*':'/angular2/*.js',

'rtts_assert/*': '/rtts_assert/*.js',
```

```
'services/*' : '/services/*.js',

'tdApp': 'TdApp.es6'

};

System.import('tdApp');

</script>

</body>

</html>
```

The app is now ready to be run. Navigate to the root directory and once you are there, just type "*http-server.*" The app can then be accessed at "*http://localhost:8080.*"However, if you have not installed the "*http-server*" on your server, run the following command so as to download and install it:

sudo npm install -g http-server

Chapter 3:
How to create forms in
AngularJS 2

While developing our applications, we need to take care of how the input will be handled. In Angular 1, you were used to the ng-model providing a nice way of how to handle the user input. However, this can be advanced as it has been done in AngularJS 2. The new module for this makes it easier for us to handle user input with the same convenience provided in the ng-model but without the drawbacks associated with the ng-model.

In AngularJS 2, forms are broken down into three layers. At the bottom of the form, we can implement the elements which belong to HTML. In the layer above this, we are are provided with the Form Control API. A data-driven forms API is also provided, and this makes it easy for us to create large forms.

When you look at it shallowly, it might seem to be a bit simple to create forms in AngularJS 1. However, there are major benefits associated by the use of AngularJS 2 for this purpose. The behavior of the form becomes different from that of the template, meaning that it will be tested independently. The process of testing and execution will have been made very easy.

Data-driven forms

Suppose that we wanted to create a form which takes up the following structure:

street

24 Lake View Street

city State Zip

New York USA 9067

☐ House

This form can be implemented by use of the code given below:

```
import {forms, required, materialDesign} from
'angular2/forms';

// the model

class Location {
```

```
        street: string;

        state: string;

        city: string;

        zip: string;

        house: boolean;

}

@Component({

        selector: 'form'

})

@Template({

// the layout of the form will be automatic depending
on structure

        inline: `<form [form-
structure]="form"></form>`

        directives: [forms]

})

class Form {
```

```
constructor(fb: FormBuilder) {

    this.location = new Location();

// let us define and initialize the structure of the form
depending on

// the model which has been passed

    this.myform = fb.fromModel(location, [

// describe the field of the model, labels and how to
handle errors

    {field: 'city', label: 'City', validator: required},

    {field: 'street', label: 'Street', validator:
required},

    {field: 'state', label: 'State', size: 2,

    validator: required},

    {field: 'zip', label: 'Zip', size: 5,

    validator: zipCodeValidator},

    {field: 'isHouse', type: 'checkbox',

    label: 'Is House'}

}, {
```

```
// the model will be updated whenever the input is
changed

    saveOnUpdate: true,

// allow to set different strategies for the layout

    lStrategy: mDesign

});

}

}

function zipCodeValidator(control) {

    if    (!    control.value.match(/\d\d\d\d\d(-
\d\d\d\d)?/)){

        return {invalidZipCode: true};

}

}
```

We have created a form. What we have done is that we have described the fields, the labels, and any other components in a very declarative way. This will give us a form. The layout of the form in an HTML form will then be produced, depending on what is passed to the builder. A look and feel which is consistent will then be kept throughout the application. The write through behavior in the form can also be controlled.

The API for the form is also pluggable, thus, we will be in a position to define custom validators, be in a position to re-use the controls of the web-component, and also define the theme and the layout.

Form Controls

It is a good idea for us to have data-driven forms. However, as developers, it is important for us to exercise full control over how the form is being laid out on the web page. We want to rebuild the above form but this time around, we want to use the low level API, and this will give us room to exercise full control of the structure of our form.

street

24 Lake View Street

city State Zip

New York USA 9067

☐ House

The code is given below:

import {forms, required} from 'angular2/forms';

// A typical model of a form- example

```
class Location {

        city: string;

        street: string;

        state: string;

        zip: string;

        house: boolean;

}

function zipCodeValidator(control) {

        if      (!       control.value.match(/\d\d\d\d\d(-
\d\d\d\d)?/)){

                return {invalidZipCode: true};

}

}

@Component({

        selector: 'form'

})

@Template({
```

inline: `

```
// let us define the template for our form explicitly.

<form [form]="form">

    Street <input control="street">

    <div                    *if="form.hasError('street',
'required')">Required</div>

State <input control="state" size="2">

    <div                    *if="form.hasError('state',
'required')">Required</div>

City <input control="city">

    <div                    *if="form.hasError('city',
'required')">Required</div>

Zip <input control="zip" size="5">

    <div                    *if="form.hasError('zip',
'invalidZipCoed')">

The Zip code is not valid

    </div>

House <input control="isHouse" type="checkbox">
```

```
</form>

        `directives: [forms]

})

class Form {

        constructor(fb: FormBuilder) {

        this.location = new Location();


// defining the model of the form

        this.myform = fb.group({

        street: [this.address.street, required],

        state: [this.address.city, required],

        city: [this.address.city, required],

        zip: [this.address.zip, zipCodeValidator],

isHouse: [this.address.isHouse]

});

thismy.form.changes.forEach(()                          =>
this.myform.writeTo(this.location));
```

```
    }

  }
```

Even though we have used the form control API, the behavior of the form has also been defined in the component. However, the layout of the form is defined in the template. This makes it possible for us to be able to implement forms which are unusual.

As shown in the two examples, the process of building forms with the new model for forms in Angular 2 is very easy and fast. It also offers a benefit in that all the forms used in the app will exhibit a look and feel which is consistent throughout. It will then be easy to test, and the behavior of the forms will be highly predictable.

Chapter 4: Directives

We said that with AngularJS 2, it is possible for us to extend the HTML. In this chapter, we will discuss how this is done. The attributes in this case start with the "*ng*" prefix. The following are the directives to be discussed:

- ng-app – responsible for starting the AngularJS application.

- ng-init – responsible for initialization of the application data.

- ng-model – responsible for defining the model, that is, variable which is to be used in the AngularJS 2.

- ng-repeat – this will repeat each of the elements which are found in the collection.

ng-app directive

This is responsible for starting the application. It also defines what the root element is. Whenever the web page containing the AngularJS application is loaded, then it will automatically initialize the application. It is also responsible for the loading of the various AngularJS 2 modules which are used in the application. It takes the syntax given below:

<div ng-app="">

...

</div>

ng-init directive

It is responsible for the initialization of the data for the AngularJS 2 application. It puts data into the respective variables of the application. Consider the following example in which we have defined an array for holding some values:

```
<div    ng-app=""    ng-init="names=[{locale:'en-J',name:'John'},

     {locale:'en-M',name:'Mike'},

     {locale:'en-N',name:'Nicholas'}]">

...

</div>
```

ng-model directive

This will define the model or the variable which is to be used in the application. Consider the example given below:

<div ng-app="">

...

<p>Provide your Name: **<input type="text" ng-model="name"></p>**

</div>

In the above example, the name of the model is *"name."*

ng-repeat directive

With this, each of the elements which are contained in the directive will be repeated. Consider the following example in which we are iterating the elements of an array:

```
<div ng-app="">

...

    <p>List of names:</p>

<ol>

    <li ng-repeat="name in names">

        {{ 'Name: ' + name.name + ', Locale: ' + name.locale }}

</li>

</ol>
```

</div>

In the example shown below, we are demonstrating how all of these can be used:

<html>

<title>AngularJS 2 Directives**</title>**

<body>

<h1>Example Application**</h1>**

<div   ng-app=""   ng-init="names=[{locale:'en-USA',name:'John'},

{locale:'en-Russia',name:'Mike'},

{locale:'en-Kenya',name:'Nicholas'}]">

<p>Provide   your   Name: **<input   type="text"   ng-model="name"></p>**

```html
<p>Hello <span ng-bind="name"></span>!</p>

<p>The following is the list of available names:</p>

<ol>

<li ng-repeat="name in names">

{{ 'Name: ' + name.name + ', Locale: ' + name.locale }}

</li>

</ol>

</div>

<script
src="http://ajax.googleapis.com/ajax/libs/angularjs/
1.3.14/angular.min.js"></script>

</body>

</html>
```

The above program will demonstrate all that we have learned practically. Just run it, and observe the output. It will be as follows:

Example Application

Provide your Name: Mike

Hello Mike!

The following is the list of available names:

1. Name: John, Locale: en-USA
2. Name: Mike, Locale: en-Russia
3. Name: Nicholas, Locale: en-Kenya

Chapter 5: Views

The view determines how the application will look like to the users. AngularJS 2 provides both the *"ng-view"* and the *"ng-template"* which can be used for this purpose.

ng-view

This will create a placeholder for placement of a corresponding view, and this is based on the configuration. It is used as shown below:

```
<div ng-app="myApp">

...

<div ng-view></div>

</div>
```

ng-template

This uses the *"script"* tag so as to create an HTML view. For the purpose of mapping the view to the controller, an *"id"* attribute is used. This is demonstrated in the example given below:

```
<div ng-app="myApp">

...

        <script                type="text/ng-template"
id="createApp.htm">

            <h2> Add app </h2>

            {{message}}

</script>


</div>
```

$routeProvider

This is the main service which is responsible for the configuration of URLs. It also maps these URLs to their corresponding ng-template or html page. A controller should also be attached.

It is used as shown below:

```
<div ng-app="myApp">

        ...

        <script                    type="text/ng-template"
id="createApp.htm">

            <h2> Create App </h2>

            {{message}}

        </script>

</div>
```

The above code shows that the *"$routeProvide"* can be used to define a script block whose type is *"ng-template."*

We can also use it to define a script block having the main module, and then set the routing configuration. This is shown below:

```
var myApp = angular.module("myApp", ['ngRoute']);

    myApp.config(['$routeProvider',

function($routeProvider) {

$routeProvider.

    when('/createApp', {

    templateUrl: 'createApp.htm',

    controller: 'CreateAppController'

}).

    when('/viewApps', {

    templateUrl: 'viewApps.htm',

    controller: 'ViewAppsController'
```

```
}).

otherwise({

        redirectTo: '/createApp'

});

}]);
```

Let us demonstrate these by use of an example. This is given below:

```html
<html>

<head>

<title>Views with AngularJS 2</title>

<script
src="http://ajax.googleapis.com/ajax/libs/angularjs/
1.3.14/angular.min.js"></script>

<script
src="http://ajax.googleapis.com/ajax/libs/angularjs/
1.3.14/angular-route.min.js"></script>

</head>

<body>
```

```html
<h2>AngularJS 2 Example Application</h2>

<div ng-app="myApp">

<p><a href="#createApp">Create App</a></p>

<p><a href="#viewApps">View Apps</a></p>

<div ng-view></div>

<script                               type="text/ng-template"
id="createApp.htm">

<h2> Create App </h2>

{{message}}

</script>

<script type="text/ng-template" id="viewApps.htm">

<h2> View Apps </h2>

{{message}}

</script>

</div>

<script>

var myApp = angular.module("myApp", ['ngRoute']);
```

```
myApp.config(['$routeProvider',

function($routeProvider) {

$routeProvider.

when('/createApp', {

templateUrl: 'createApp.htm',

controller: 'CreateAppsController'

}).

when('/viewApps', {

templateUrl: 'viewApps.htm',

controller: 'ViewAppsController'

}).

otherwise({

redirectTo: '/createApp'

});

}]);

myApp.controller('CreatePersonController',
function($scope) {
```

```
$scope.message = "This page will provide the page for
creating a new app";

});

myApp.controller('ViewAppsController',
function($scope) {

$scope.message = "All the available apps will be
displayed on this page";

});

</script>

</body>

</html>
```

The program has demonstrated how to use all the features
which we have discussed in this chapter. Just write it as it is,
and then run it. You will observe the following output:

AngularJS 2 Example Application

Create App

View Apps

Create App

Chapter 6:
Expressions in AngularJS 2

These are used for the purpose of binding the data for the application to html. To indicate an expression, we use double curly braces, that is, ({{}}). The expression is placed in between these. Their behavior is related to that of the *"ng-bind"* directives. They take the syntax of Javascript, and they will only output data where they have been used.

To use them with numbers, we follow the syntax below:

<p>Expense on Food: {{cost * quantity}} Rs</p>

When used with strings, the syntax below is adhered to:

<p>Hello {{person.fname + " " + person.lname}}!</p>

In objects, the following is the syntax:

<p>Roll No: {{teacher.rollno}}</p>

For arrays, the following is the syntax:

```
<p>Marks(English): {{marks[4]}}</p>
```

Let us use an example to demonstrate how all the above expressions are used:

```
<html>

<title> Expressions  in AngularJS 2</title>

<body>

<h1>Example Application</h1>

<div ng-app="" ng-init="quantity=1;cost=30;

person={firstname:'Mike',lastname:'Artemov',age:35
};contribution=[70,80,34,67,90]">

<p>Hello {{person.firstname + " " + person.lastname}}!</p>

<p>Total contribution is : {{cost * quantity}} Rs</p>
```

```
<p>Age: {{person.age}}</p>

<p>Contribution(First): {{contribution[3]}}</p>

</div>

<script
src="http://ajax.googleapis.com/ajax/libs/angularjs/
1.3.14/angular.min.js"></script>

</body>

</html>
```

Just write the program as it has been written above. Save and then run it. You will get the following as the output:

Example Application

Hello Mike Artemov!

Total contribution is : 30 Rs

Age: 35

Contribution(First): 67

Chapter 7: Filters

The purpose of filters is to modify data, and can be used together with directives and expressions by use of the pipe character. The following are some of the filters which are commonly used:

- Uppercase- converts a text which is in lowercase to uppercase.

- Lowercase- converts a text which is in uppercase to lowercase.

- Currency- the specified text is formatted into a currency format.

- Filter- it is used to filter the components of an array based on the criterion which has been specified.

- Orderby- the elements of the array are filtered based on the criteria which has been specified.

Uppercase filter

This filter is added to an expression by use of the pipe character. Consider the example given below:

Provide first name:<input type="text" ng-model="person.fName">

Provide last name: <input type="text" ng-model="person.lName">

Name in Upper Case: {{person.fullName() | uppercase}}

With the above example, all the names of the persons will be printed in uppercase.

lowercase filter

This should be added to the expression by use of the pipe character. Consider the example given below:

Provide first name:<input type="text" ng-model="person.fName">

Provide last name: <input type="text" ng-model="person.lName">

Name in Upper Case: {{person.fullName() | lowercase}}

With the above filter, all the names of the persons will be printed in lowercase.

Currency filter

This can be applied to any expression which is expected to return a number by use of the pipe character. Consider the example given below:

Enter salary: <input type="text" ng-model="person.salary">

salary: {{person.salary | currency}}

With the above filter, the salary of the person will be printed in a currency format.

Filter filter

This is used when you wish to display only a subset of the elements. Consider the following example:

Provide specialization: <input type="text" ng-model="sName">

Specialization:

<ul>

<li ng-repeat="specialization of the worker.fields | filter: sName">

{{ specialization.name + ', salary:' + specialization.salary }}

</li>

</ul>

orderBy filter

We need to order the employees by their salaries. This is shown below:

Specialization:

<ul>

<li ng-repeat="specialization in field.fields | orderBy:'salary'">

{{ specialization.name + ', salary:' + specialization.salary }}

</li>

</ul>

We now need to demonstrate how all of the above can be done by use of an example. Consider the following:

<html>

<head>

```html
<title>Filters in AngularJS 2</title>

<script
src="http://ajax.googleapis.com/ajax/libs/angularjs/
1.3.14/angular.min.js"></script>

</head>

<body>

<h2>AngularJS 2 Example Application</h2>

<div                ng-app="myApp"              ng-
controller="personController">

<table border="0">

<tr><td>Provide     first     name:</td><td><input
type="text" ng-model="person.fName"></td></tr>

<tr><td>Provide     last     name:    </td><td><input
type="text" ng-model="person.lName"></td></tr>

<tr><td>Provide      Salary:       </td><td><input
type="text" ng-model="person.salary"></td></tr>

<tr><td>Provide    Specialization:   </td><td><input
type="text" ng-model="sName"></td></tr>

</table>
```

```html
<br/>

<table border="0">

<tr><td>Name in Upper Case: </td><td>{{person.fullName() | uppercase}}</td></tr>

<tr><td>Name in Lower Case: </td><td>{{person.fullName() | lowercase}}</td></tr>

<tr><td>salary: </td><td>{{person.salary | currency}}</td></tr>

<tr><td>Specialization:</td><td>

<ul>

<li ng-repeat="specialization in person.fields | filter: sName |orderBy:'salary'">

{{ specialization.name + ', salary:' + specialization.salary }}

</li>

</ul>

</td></tr>

</table>
```

```
</div>

<script>

var myApp = angular.module("myApp", []);

myApp.controller('personController',
function($scope) {

$scope.person = {

fName: "Mike",

lName: "Artemov",

salary:5000,

specialization:[

{name:'Programmer',salary:2500},

{name:'Networker',salary:1000},

{name:'Administrator',salary:1500}

],

fullName: function() {

var personObject;

personObject = $scope.person;
```

```
return        personObject.fName        +      "      "      +
personObject.lName;

}

};

});

</script>

</body>

</html>
```

Just write the program, and then run it. You will observe the following as the output:

AngularJS 2 Example Application

Provide first name: Mike

Provide last name: Artemov

Provide Salary: 5000

Provide Specialization:

Name in Upper Case: MIKE ARTEMOV

Name in Lower Case: mike artemov

salary: $5,000.00

Specialization:

Every kind of filer has worked as it is shown in the above figure.

Chapter 8: Controllers

This framework relies on the controllers for the purpose of controlling how the data flows in the application. To define the controller, we use the *"ng-controller"* directive. The controller will contain the functions and attributes/properties for our application. Each of our controllers will accept the parameter *"$scope"* which will refer to the module/application which the controller is expected to control. The following syntax is used:

<div ng-app="" ng-controller="personController">

...

</div>

In the above example, we have used the *"ng-controller"* directive so as to declare our controller, and we have given it the name *"personController."* After the next step, we should have the following:

```
<script>

function personController($scope) {

    $scope.person = {

    fName: "Mike",

    lName: "Artemov",

    fullName: function() {

    var personObject;

    personObject = $scope.person;

return        personObject.fName       +       "       "       +
personObject.lName;

    }};

}

</script>
```

The *"personController"* has been defined like a Javascript object, and the argument used in this case is *"$scope."* The application which is intended to use the object *"personController"* is the one being referred to by the *"$scope."* The *"$scope.person"* is a property of the object *"personController." "fName"* and *"lName"* are also properties, and we have given them some default values. Let us demonstrate this by the use of an example as shown below:

```
<html>

<head>

<title>Angular JS Controller</title>

<script
src="http://ajax.googleapis.com/ajax/libs/angularjs/
1.3.14/angular.min.js"></script>

</head>

<body>

<h2>AngularJS 2 Example Application</h2>

<div ng-app="myApp" ng-
controller="personController">
```

Provide first name: <input type="text" ng-model="person.fName">

Provide last name: <input type="text" ng-model="person.lName">

You have entered: {{person.fullName()}}

</div>

<script>

var myApp = angular.module("myApp", []);

myApp.controller('personController', function($scope) {

$scope.person = {

fName: "Mike",

lName: "Artemov",

fullName: function() {

var personObject;

personObject = $scope.person;

```
return    personObject.firstName    +    "    "    +
personObject.lastName;

}

};

});

</script>

</body>

</html>
```

Just write the above program, and then run it. You will get the

following output:

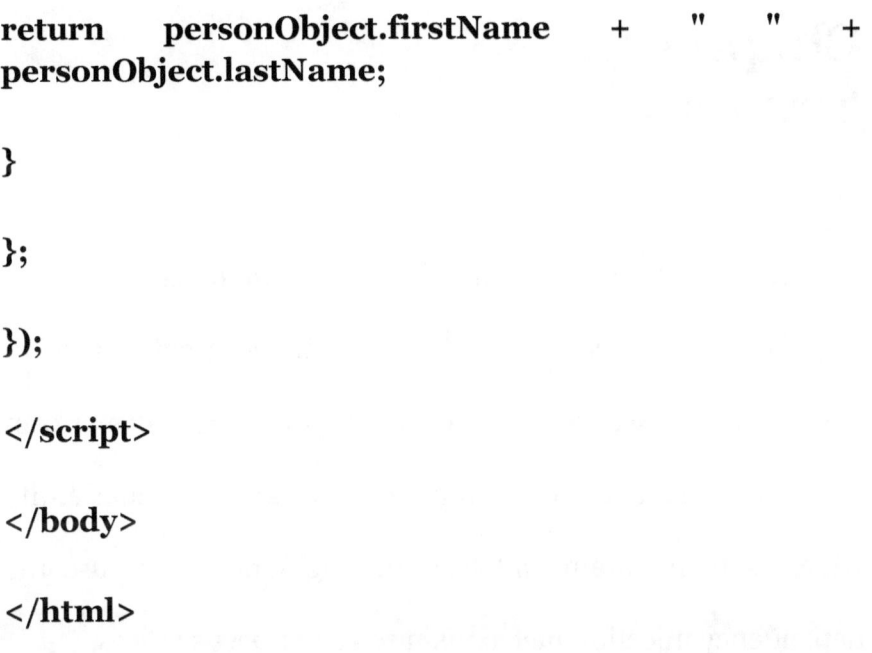

AngularJS 2 Example Application

Provide first name: Mike

Provide last name: Artemov

You have entered: Mike Artemov

Chapter 9: Services

By the use of the concept of *"separation of concerns"* in AngularJS 2, we come up with the service architecture. In Javascript, services are a kind of functions that can perform only one task. This means that they are an individual entity which is to maintain and test. In AngularJS 2, we use the dependency injection mechanism so as to inject services.

AngularJS 2 comes with numerous services which are built-in, such as the $location, $route, $http, $window, and others. Each task is associated with a specific task, for example, *"$route"* is used for the purpose of defining routing information. *"$http"* is used for the making of a call to the ajax so as to get data from the server.

There are two ways in which a service can be created. These are:

- Service
- Factory
  -

Factory method

With this method, we begin by defining a factory, and then a method is assigned to it. This is shown below:

```
var myApp = angular.module("myApp", []);

    myApp.factory('MathService', function() {

        var fact = {};

        fact.multiply = function(x, y) {

            return x * y

}

return fact;

});
```

Service method

In this method, a service is defined, and then a method is assigned to it. A service which is already in existence should also be injected. Consider the example given below:

```
myApp.service('CalculationService',
function(MathService){

        this.sq= function(x) {

        return MathService.multiply(x,x);

}

});
```

The following example shows how the above can be used:

```
<html>

<head>

<title>AngularJS 2 Services</title>
```

```html
<script
src="http://ajax.googleapis.com/ajax/libs/angularjs/
1.3.14/angular.min.js"></script>

</head>

<body>

<h2>AngularJS 2 Example Application</h2>

<div                ng-app="myApp"                ng-
controller="CalculationController">

<p>Provide a number: <input type="number" ng-
model="number" />

<button                                            ng-
click="square()">X<sup>2</sup></button>

<p>Answer: {{result}}</p>

</div>

<script>

var myApp = angular.module("myApp", []);

myApp.factory('MathService', function() {

var fact = {};

fact.multiply = function(x, y) {
```

```javascript
return x * y

}

return fact;

});

myApp.service('CalculationService',
function(MathService){

this.square = function(x) {

return MathService.multiply(x,x);

}

});

myApp.controller('CalculationController',
function($scope, CalculationService) {

$scope.square = function() {

$scope.result                                    =
CalculationService.square($scope.number);

}

});

</script>
```

</body>

</html>

Just write the above program as it is, and then execute it. You will see the following interface:

AngularJS 2 Example Application

Provide a number: [   ] [⇕] [X²]

Answer:

The application should function like a calculator. Just enter a number as you are directed, and then click on the right-most button. This is demonstrated below:

AngularJS 2 Example Application

Provide a number: 6 [   ] [⇕] [X²]

Answer:

As shown in the above figure, I have provided the number 6 in the text field. On pressing the right-most button, I get the following:

AngularJS 2 Example Application

Provide a number: 6   X²

Answer: 36

As shown in the figure, the program gives the square of the number.

Chapter 10:
Tables

The nature of table data is that it is repeated. This is why we use the *"ng-repeat"* to easily draw tables in AngularJS 2. This is used as follows:

```
<table>

<tr>

        <th>Name</th>

        <th>Salary</th>

        </tr>

        <tr     ng-repeat="specialization     in
person.fields">

                <td>{{ specialization.name }}</td>

                        <td>{{      specialization.salary
}}</td>

</tr>
```

```
</table>
```

To style the table, we use CSS as follows:

```
<style>

        table, th , td {

        border: 1px solid grey;

        border-collapse: collapse;

        padding: 5px;

}

table tr:nth-child(odd) {

        background-color: #fff2f2;

}

table tr:nth-child(even) {

        background-color: #f2f2ff;

}

</style>
```

Let us demonstrate this by use of an example. This is given below:

```html
<html>

<head>

<title>AngularJS 2 Table</title>

<script
src="http://ajax.googleapis.com/ajax/libs/angularjs/
1.3.14/angular.min.js"></script>

<style>

table, th , td {

border: 2px solid grey;

border-collapse: collapse;

padding: 4px;

}

table tr:nth-child(odd) {

background-color: #fff2f2;
```

```
}

table tr:nth-child(even) {

background-color: #f2f2ff;

}

</style>

</head>

<body>

<h2>AngularJS 2 Example Application</h2>

<div                ng-app="myApp"                ng-
controller="personController">

<table border="0">

<tr><td>Provide      first       name:</td><td><input
type="text" ng-model="person.fName"></td></tr>

<tr><td>Provide      last      name:   </td><td><input
type="text" ng-model="person.lName"></td></tr>

<tr><td>Name:
</td><td>{{person.fullName()}}</td></tr>

<tr><td>Specialization:</td><td>
```

```
<table>

<tr>

<th>Name</th>

<th>Salary</th>

</tr>

<tr ng-repeat="subject in person.fields">

<td>{{ specialization.name }}</td>

<td>{{ specialization.salary }}</td>

</tr>

</table>

</td></tr>

</table>

</div>

<script>

var myApp = angular.module("myApp", []);

myApp.controller('personController',
function($scope) {
```

```javascript
$scope.person = {

fName: "Mike",

lName: "Artemov",

salary:5000,

fields:[

{name:'Programming',salary:2000},

{name:'Networking',salary:1000},

{name:'Administration',salary:100},

{name:'Accounting',salary:800},

{name:'Sales',salary:200}

],

fullName: function() {

var personObject;

personObject = $scope.person;

return        personObject.fName      +      "      "      +
personObject.lName;

}
```

```
};

});

</script>

</body>

</html>
```

Just write the program as it is shown above, and then run it.

You will get the following result as the output:

AngularJS 2 Example Application

Provide first name:	Mike	
Provide last name:	Artemov	
Name:	Mike Artemov	
Specialization:	**Name**	**Salary**

Chapter 11:
HTML DOM

In AngularJS 2, we can use directives so as to bind the data for the application to the HTML DOM Elements. These directives include the following:

- ng-disabled- used for disabling a given control.

- ng-show- used to show a given control.

- ng-hide- used for hiding a given control.

- ng-click- used to represent an AngularJS click event.

ng-disabled directive

This attribute should be added to an HTML button, and then passed to a model. The model should then be bound to a checkbox, and the variation observed. This is shown below:

<input type="checkbox" ng-model="enableDisableButton"> Button 1

<button ng-disabled="enableDisableButton">Click Here!</button>

ng-show directive

This should also be added to an HTML button, and then passed to a model. The model should then be bound to a checkbox and the variation observed. This is shown below:

<input type="checkbox" ng-model="showHide1">Button 2

<button ng-show="showHide1">Click Here!</button>

ng-hide directive

This should also be added to an HTML button, and then passed to a model. The model should then be bound to a checkbox, and the variation observed. This is shown below:

<input type="checkbox" ng-model="showHide2"> Button 3

<button ng-hide="showHide2">Click Here!</button>

ng-click directive

This attribute should be added to an HTML button, and then the model updated. The model should then be bound to html, and the variation observed. This is shown below:

<p>Number of clicks: {{ clickCounter }}</p></td>

<button ng-click="clickCounter = clickCounter + 1">Click Here!</button>

We now want to use an example so as to demonstrate how the above directives can be used. This is given below:

<html>

```html
<head>

<title>AngularJS 2 HTML DOM</title>

</head>

<body>

<h2>AngularJS 2 Example Application</h2>

<div ng-app="">

<table border="0">

<tr>

<td><input type="checkbox" ng-model="enableDisableButton">Disable Button</td>

<td><button ng-disabled="enableDisableButton">Click Here!</button></td>

</tr>

<tr>
```

```
<td><input type="checkbox" ng-
model="showHide1"> Button 1</td>

<td><button ng-show="showHide1">Click
Here!</button></td>

</tr>

<tr>

<td><input type="checkbox" ng-
model="showHide2"> Button 2</td>

<td><button ng-hide="showHide2">Click
Here!</button></td>

</tr>

<tr>

<td><p>Number of clicks: {{ clickCounter
}}</p></td>

<td><button ng-click="clickCounter = clickCounter +
1">Click Here!</button></td>

</tr>

</table>

</div>
```

```
<script
src="http://ajax.googleapis.com/ajax/libs/angularjs/
1.3.14/angular.min.js"></script>

</body>

</html>
```

Just write the program as it is, and then run it. You will

observe the following as the output:

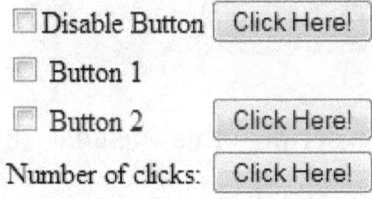

AngularJS 2 Example Application

☐ Disable Button Click Here!
☐ Button 1
☐ Button 2 Click Here!
Number of clicks: Click Here!

The output is made up of three buttons. On clicking the last

button, you will notice that the number of counts will be

incremented by 1 on each increment.

Chapter 12: Includes

With AngularJS 2, it is not possible for you to embed an html page inside another html page. However, it is possible that you might want to achieve this functionality. It can be done as follows:

- By use of Ajax- we call the server so as to get the corresponding html page. This is then set in the innerHTML of the HTML control.

- By use of server side scripts- this includes the use of server side technologies such as PHP, JSP, and others so as to include html pages in a dynamic web page.

The directive *"ng-include"* is used for including an HTML page within an HTML page. This is shown below:

<div ng-app="" ng-controller="personController">

```html
<div ng-include="'main.htm'"></div>

<div ng-include="'fields.htm'"></div>

</div>
```

Let us illustrate this by use of an example program. This is shown below:

```html
<html>

<head>

<title>AngularJS 2 Includes</title>

<script
src="http://ajax.googleapis.com/ajax/libs/angularjs/
1.3.14/angular.min.js"></script>

<style>

table, th , td {

border: 2px solid grey;

border-collapse: collapse;
```

```css
padding: 4px;

}

table tr:nth-child(odd) {

background-color: #fffff2;

}

table tr:nth-child(even) {

background-color: #f2f2ff;

}
```

```html
</style>

</head>

<body>

<h2>AngularJS 2 Example Application</h2>

<div                ng-app="myApp"                ng-controller="personController">

<div ng-include="'main.htm'"></div>

<div ng-include="'fields.htm'"></div>

</div>
```

```
<script>

var myApp = angular.module("myApp", []);

myApp.controller('personController',
function($scope) {

$scope.person = {

fName: "Mike",

lName: "Artemov",

salary:5000,

fields:[

{name:'Programming',salary:2000},

{name:'Networking',salary:1000},

{name:'Administration',salary:100},

{name:'Accounting',salary:800},

{name:'Sales',salary:200}

],

fullName: function() {

var personObject;
```

```
personObject = $scope.person;

return       personObject.fName    +    "    "    +
personObject.lName;

}

};

});

</script>

</body>

</html>
```

The file *"main.html"* should be as follows:

```
<table border="0">

<tr><td>Provide       first       name:</td><td><input
type="text" ng-model="person.fName"></td></tr>

<tr><td>Provide    last    name:    </td><td><input
type="text" ng-model="person.lName"></td></tr>

<tr><td>Name:
</td><td>{{person.fullName()}}</td></tr>
```

```
</table>
```

The file *"fields.html"* should be as follows:

```
<p>Fields:</p>

        <table>

<tr>

        <th>Name</th>

        <th>Salary</th>

</tr>

        <tr        ng-repeat="specialization        in
person.fields">

        <td>{{ [specialization.name }}</td>

        <td>{{ specialization.salary }}</td>

</tr>

</table>
```

Once all your files are ready, you can then run the application. To run it, all the above files need to be deployed in the webserver. After the deployment, you can access the first file which we created by opening it in the web browser.

Chapter 13:
Modules

The modular approach is supported in AngularJS 2. With this, the programmers find it easy for them to separate logic such as the controllers, services, application, and others. The code is also kept very clean. What happens is that they are defined in their own and a different file and given the name *"module.js."* The following are some of the modules which can be created:

- Application Module – with this, the application is initialized by the use of controllers.

- Controller Module- this is used for the definition of the controller.

Application module

This can be used as follows:

var myApp = angular.module("myApp", []);

What we have done is that we have declared the module for the application *"myApp."* We have used the function *"angular.module"* to do this. We have also passed an array which is empty to it. The modules for the array are dependent.

Controller module

Consider the Javascript program shown below:

```javascript
myApp.controller("personController",
function($scope) {

$scope.person = {

fName: "Mike",

lName: "Artemov",

salary:5000,

fields:[

{name:'Programming',salary:2000},

{name:'Networking',salary:1000},

{name:'Administration',salary:100},

{name:'Accounting',salary:800},

{name:'Sales',salary:200}

],
```

```
fullName: function() {

var personObject;

personObject = $scope.person;

return     personObject.fName     +     "     "     +
personObject.lName;

}

};


});
```

In the above program, we have used the function *"myApp.controller"* so as to declare our controller.

Use modules

Consider the program code given below:

```
<div ng-app="myApp" ng-
controller="personController">

    ..

    <script src="myApp.js"></script>

    <script src="personController.js"></script>
```

In the above code, the application-module has been included in the app by use of the *"ng-app"* directive while the controller is included by use of the *"ng-controller"* module. *"myApp"* and the *"personController"* have also been imported in the above code.

Let us demonstrate how this can be done by use of a program. This is given below:

```html
<html>

<head>

<title>AngularJS 2 Modules</title>

<script
src="http://ajax.googleapis.com/ajax/libs/angularjs/
1.3.14/angular.min.js"></script>

<script src="myApp.js"></script>

<script src="personController.js"></script>

<style>

table, th , td {

border: 1px solid grey;

border-collapse: collapse;

padding: 5px;

}

table tr:nth-child(odd) {

background-color: #fffff2;

}
```

```
table tr:nth-child(even) {

background-color: #f2f2ff;

}

</style>

</head>

<body>

<h2>AngularJS Sample Application</h2>

<div                ng-app="myApp"               ng-
controller="personController">

<table border="0">

<tr><td>Provide    first    name:</td><td><input
type="text" ng-model="person.fName"></td></tr>

<tr><td>Provide   last   name:   </td><td><input
type="text" ng-model="person.lName"></td></tr>

<tr><td>Name:
</td><td>{{person.fullName()}}</td></tr>

<tr><td>Specialization:</td><td>

<table>
```

```html
<tr>

<th>Name</th>

<th>Salary</th>

</tr>

<tr ng-repeat="subject in person.fields">

<td>{{ specialization.name }}</td>

<td>{{ specialization.salary }}</td>

</tr>

</table>

</td></tr>

</table>

</div>

</body>

</html>
```

The code for the file "*myApp.js*" should be as follows:

```javascript
var myApp = angular.module("myApp", []);
```

The code for the file *"personController.js"* should be as follows:

```
myApp.controller("personController",
function($scope) {

        $scope.person = {

        fName: "Mike",

        lName: "Artemov",

        salary:5000,

        fields:[

        {name:'Programming',salary:2000},

        {name:'Networking',salary:1000},

        {name:'Administration',salary:100},

        {name:'Accounting',salary:800},

        {name:'Sales',salary:200}

        ],

fullName: function() {
```

```
    var personObject;

    personObject = $scope.person;

            return personObject.fName  +  "  "  +
personObject.lName;

}

};

});
```

Open the first file which we created in your browser, and then
observe the result that you get. It should be as follows:

AngularJS 2 Example Application

Provide first name:	Mike	
Provide last name:	Artemov	
Name:	Mike Artemov	
Specialization:	Name	Salary

Chapter 14: Scopes

In Javascript, scope is a special object which can be used to join together the views and the controllers. It has the data for the model. If you are in a controller and you want to access the data for the model, use the object "*$scope.*" This is shown below:

```
<script>

        var myApp = angular.module("myApp", []);

        myApp.controller("shapeController",
function($scope) {

        $scope.message = "The shape controller";

        $scope.type = "Shape";

});

</script>
```

With the above example, it is good for you to note the following points:

- "*$scope*" has been passed as the first argument to the controller at the time of defining the constructor.

- "*$scope.type*" and "*$scope.model*" are the models to be passed in the HTML page.

- Functions can also be defined in the "*$scope.*"

Scope Inheritance

You need to note that scope is specific to a controller. After defining nested controllers, what will happen is that the child controller inherits the parent controller. This is demonstrated in the program given below:

```
<script>

        var myApp = angular.module("myApp", []);

        myApp.controller("shapeController",
function($scope) {

        $scope.message = "The shape controller";

        $scope.type = "Shape";

});

myApp.controller("circleController",
function($scope) {

        $scope.message = "The circle controller";

});
```

</script>

With the above example, the following points are important to be noted:

- The values for the model have been set in the *"shapeController."*

- The message has been overridden in the child controller *"circleController."*

Let us demonstrate how the above directives can be used by the use of an example:

<html>

<head>

<title>AngularJS 2 Forms</title>

</head>

<body>

```html
<h2>AngularJS 2 Example Application</h2>

<div ng-app="myApp" ng-controller="shapeController">

<p>{{msg}} <br/> {{type}} </p>

<div ng-controller="circleController">

<p>{{msg}} <br/> {{type}} </p>

</div>

<div ng-controller="squareController">

<p>{{msg}} <br/> {{type}} </p>

</div>

</div>

<script src="http://ajax.googleapis.com/ajax/libs/angularjs/1.3.14/angular.min.js"></script>

<script>

var myApp = angular.module("myApp", []);

myApp.controller("shapeController", function($scope) {
```

```
$scope.msg = "The shape controller";

$scope.type = "Shape";

});

myApp.controller("circleController",
function($scope) {

$scope.msg = "The circle controller";

});

myApp.controller("squareController",
function($scope) {

$scope.msg = "The square controller";

$scope.type = "Square";

});

</script>

</body>

</html>
```

Just write the program as it is written, and then execute or run it. You will notice the following result as the output:

AngularJS 2 Example Application

The shape controller
Shape

The circle controller
Shape

The square controller
Square

Chapter 15:
Custom Directives

These are used for the purpose of extending HTML. They seem to be advanced or customized, compared to what we have in the normal directives. To define these, we use the function *"directive."* Once it has been activated, it just replaces the element it was activated for. With AngularJS 2, custom directives are provided for creating the following types of elements:

- Element directives- whenever a matching element is found, this directive is activated.

- Attribute- whenever a matching element is found, this directive is activated.

- CSS- in case a matching CSS style is encountered, then this directive is activated.

- Comment- in case a matching comment is encountered, then this directive will be activated.

How to understand Custom Directive

Begin by defining the custom html tags. This is shown below:

**<person name ="Mike"> </person>
**

<person name ="Artemov"> </person>

A custom directive for defining the above html tags should then be defined. This is shown below:

var myApp = angular.module("myApp", []);

//Creating the directive, the first parameter should be the html element which is to be attached.

//A person html tag is to be attached.

//after a person element has been encountered in the html, then the directive will be activated.

myApp.directive('person', function() {

```javascript
//defining the directive object

        var d = {};

//restrict = E, this is to signify that the directive is an
Element directive

        d.restrict = 'E';

//the template will replace the complete element with
the text.

        d.template              =              "Person:
<b>{{person.name}}</b>          ,          Age:
<b>{{person.age}}</b>";

//scope will distinguish each person element
according to the criteria.

d.scope = {

        person : "=name"

}

//compile will be called during initialization of the
application. It will be called once by the AngularJS 2
after the html page is loaded.

        d.compile = function(elmnt, attributes) {

        elmnt.css("border", "1px solid #cffccc");
```

//lFunction will be linked to each element having scope to obtain the data specific to an element.

```
        var lFunction = function($scope, elmnt,
attributes) {

        elmnt.html("Person:
<b>"+$scope.person.name        +"</b>        ,        Age:
<b>"+$scope.person.age+"</b><br/>");

        elmnt.css("background-color", "#fc00ff");

}

return lFunction;

}

        return d;

});
```

Define a controller for updating the scope of the directive. We will use the value of the attribute as the child scope.

```
myApp.controller('PersonController',
function($scope) {
```

```
$scope.Mike = {};

$scope.Mike.name = "Mike Artemov";

$scope.Mike.age  = 35;

$scope.Nicholas = {};

$scope.Nicholas.name = "Nicholas Samuel";

$scope.Nicholas.age  = 28;

});
```

This is demonstrated in the example given below:

```html
<html>

<head>

<title>AngularJS 2 Custom Directives</title>

</head>

<body>

<h2>AngularJS 2 Example Application</h2>

<div ng-app="myApp" ng-
controller="PersonController">
```

```html
<person name="Mike"></person><br/>

<person name="Nicholas"></person>

</div>

<script
src="http://ajax.googleapis.com/ajax/libs/angularjs/
1.3.14/angular.min.js"></script>

<script>

var myApp = angular.module("myApp", []);

myApp.directive('person', function() {

var d = {};

d.restrict = 'E';

d.template = "Person: <b>{{person.name}}</b> ,
Age: <b>{{person.age}}</b>";

d.scope = {

person : "=name"

}

d.compile = function(elmnt, attributes) {

elmnt.css("border", "2px solid #cccccc");
```

```javascript
var lFunction = function($scope, elmnt, attributes) {

elmnt.html("Person: <b>"+$scope.person.name
+"</b> , Age:
<b>"+$scope.person.age+"</b><br/>");


elmnt.css("background-color", "#fff0ff");

}

return lFunction;

}

return d;

});

myApp.controller('PersonController',
function($scope) {

$scope.Mike = {};

$scope.Mike.name = "Mike Artemov";

$scope.Mike.age  = 35;

$scope.Nicholas = {};

$scope.Nicholas.name = "Nicholas Samuel";
```

```
$scope.Nicholas.age  = 28;

});

</script>

</body>

</html>
```

Just write the program, and then run it. You will observe the following output:

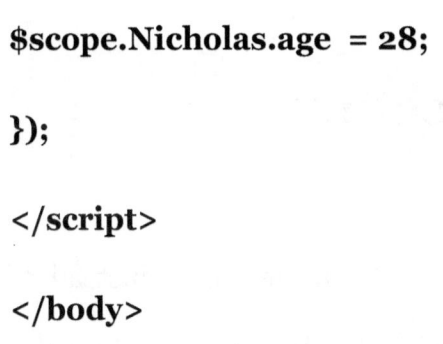

AngularJS 2 Example Application

Person: Mike Artemov, Age:35

Person: Nicholas Samuel, Age:28

The program has worked effectively.

Chapter 16:
Dependency Injection

This is a pattern for designing patterns in which instead of hard coding them into the application, we just specify their dependencies. The overall result of this is that it will be easy for us to configure the dependencies, and the components will have been relieved from the task of locating the dependencies. The components are also made easy to test, reuse, and maintain.

With AngularJS 2, we can achieve an Injection mechanism which is a supreme dependency. It has the following components which can be injected into each other as dependencies:

- constant

- service

- value

- provider

- factory

Value

This is a very simple object in Javascript, and is used for passing of values to the controller during the configuration phase. This is demonstrated below:

//defining the module

var myApp = angular.module("myApp", []);

//creating a value object as the "defaultInput" and then pass it as data.

myApp.value("defaultInput", 10);

...

//injecting the above value into the controller by use of its name "defaultInput"

myApp.controller('CalculationController', function($scope, CalcService, defaultInput) {

$scope.num = defaultInput;

$scope.answer   = CalcService.square($scope.num);

$scope.square = function() {

$scope.answer = CalcService.square($scope.num);

}

});

Factory

This is a value which can be used to return a value. A value is created whenever it is needed by the controller or the service. A factory function is normally used for calculation and returning of the value. This is shown below:

//defining the module

var myApp = angular.module("myApp", []);

//creating the factory "MathService" which will provide us with the *"multiply"* method which will return the multiplication of two numbers

myApp.factory('MathService', function() {

```
        var fact = {};

fact.multiply = function(x, y) {

        return x * y

}

        return fact;

});

//injecting the "MathService" factory into a service
for utilizing the multiply method of factory.

myApp.service('CalcService', function(MathService){

        this.square = function(x) {

        return MathService.multiply(x,x);

}

});

        ...
```

Service

This is a single object in Javascript which has a set of functions for performing certain tasks. To define these, we use the function *"service()"* and then we inject them into the controllers. Consider the demonstration given below:

//defining the module

var myApp = angular.module("myApp", []);

  ...

//creating a service which will define the square method for returning the square of a number.

```
myApp.service('CalcService', function(MathService){

        this.square = function(x) {

                return MathService.multiply(x, x);

}

});
```

```
//injecting the service "CalcService" into our
controller

myApp.controller('CalculationController',
function($scope, CalcService, defaultInput) {

        $scope.num = defaultInput;

        $scope.answer                              =
CalcService.square($scope.num);

        $scope.square = function() {

        $scope.answer                              =
CalcService.square($scope.num);

}

});
```

Provider

This is internally used by AngularJS 2 for creation of factory, services, and others at the configuration phase. It is closely related to the *"factory()"* method and it uses the *"get()"* method for returning values. This is shown below:

//defining the module

var myApp = angular.module("myApp", []);

...

//creating a service by use of a provider which will define the square method for returning the square of a number.

myApp.config(function($provide) {

    $provide.provider('MathService', function() {

        this.$get = function() {

        var fact = {};

fact.multiply = function(x, y) {

    return x * y;

}

    return fact;

};

});

});

The purpose of constants is to pass the values during the configuration phase, although you are aware that values cannot be passed at the configuration phase. This is shown below:

myApp.constant("configParam", " A constant value");

Let us demonstrate all of these directives by use of an example. This is shown below:

<html>

<head>

```html
<title>AngularJS 2 Dependency Injection</title>

</head>

<body>

<h2>AngularJS 2 Example Application</h2>

<div ng-app="myApp" ng-controller="CalculationController">

<p>Provide a number: <input type="number" ng-model="number" />

<button ng-click="square()">X<sup>2</sup></button>

<p>Answer: {{answer}}</p>

</div>

<script src="http://ajax.googleapis.com/ajax/libs/angularjs/1.3.14/angular.min.js"></script>

<script>

var myApp = angular.module("myApp", []);

myApp.config(function($provide) {

$provide.provider('MathService', function() {
```

```
this.$get = function() {

var fact = {};

fact.multiply = function(x, y) {

return x * y;

}

return fact;

};

});

});


myApp.value("defaultInput", 10);


mApp.factory('MathService', function() {

var fact = {};

fact.multiply = function(x, y) {

return x * y;
```

```
}

return fact;

});

myApp.service('CalcService', function(MathService){

this.square = function(x) {

return MathService.multiply(x, x);

}

});

myApp.controller('CalculationController',
function($scope, CalcService, defaultInput) {

$scope.num = defaultInput;

$scope.answer = CalcService.square($scope.num);

$scope.square = function() {

$scope.answer = CalcService.square($scope.num);

}

});

</script>
```

```
</body>

</html>
```

After running the program, you will notice the following output:

AngularJS 2 Example Application

Provide a number: [   ] x^2

Answer:

The application should give the square of a number. Just try it.

Conclusion

It can be concluded that AngularJS is a Javascript framework used by web developers for the development of dynamic web pages. The framework is very small in terms of size, as it is only about 60 KB. The framework is also very compatible with other Javascript frameworks, such as the EmberJS. Web pages which have been developed by use of this Javascript framework exhibit a high degree of compatibility with all the available kinds of browsers. In this case, HTML is used as the template for the web pages. This means that it forms the interface components.

Recently, the Javascript development team released AngularJS 2. This framework was developed to assist Javascript developers to create mobile apps with much ease. The framework can also be used for the development of web applications. The framework brought about much change and improvement as far as AngularJS is concerned. For instance, this framework has made the process of developing forms very easy and fast.

The framework also introduced the concept of components, which are closely related to the directives. Note that the component is made up of the views and the controllers, whereby the views form the interface while the controllers act as the directors of the flow of data within the programmer's app. The framework also supports the concept of filters, which are used to display or work on a subset of the data, such as the elements contained in an array or collection. My hope is that you have read this book and you are now an expert in using this framework for development purposes.

www.ingramcontent.com/pod-product-compliance
Lightning Source LLC
Chambersburg PA
CBHW051216170526
45166CB00005B/1917